This journal belongs to

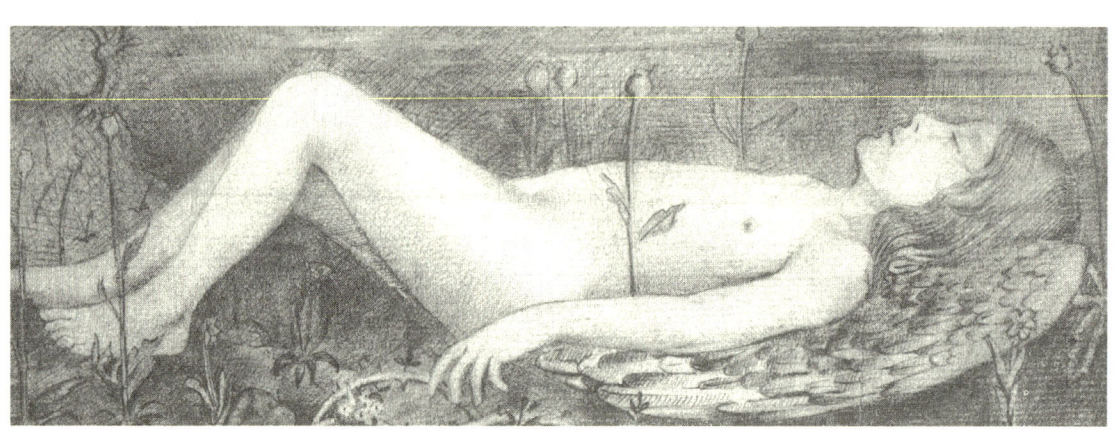

The works of Kahlil Gibran are profoundly moving in their honesty. His brushstrokes depict anguish and bliss with equal care so we can see them as equally beautiful. So, too, his words take us outside the need to transcend, control or deny our sorrows or to strive only for joy. Gibran inspires us to marvel that our emotions can be chaotic, cosmic, chasmic and climactic, and ask, "What miracle is this, that a rich and boundless universe of feeling could exist within a limited physical being?"

This journal is a place you can savour and honour your inner world, in its entirety. And also, to be inspired to authenticity. When we have only ourselves as witness, honesty may be assumed. But still, it can take practice, examination and acceptance. So, be gentle and patient as you allow genuine expression to arise and spill forth on these pages. Sketches, poetry, memories, or whatever else you gift to each leaf, do so truthfully and without the desire to understand or be understood. For, Gibran tells us that to be understood, we must limit ourselves.

Grant yourself the freedom and delight of not being grasped, of being misunderstood. Go beyond the margins. Be limitless!

Thus, I became a madman. And I have found both freedom of loneliness and the safety from being understood, for those who understand us enslave something in us.

My friend, I am not what I seem. Seeming is but a garment I wear—
a care-woven garment that protects me from thy questionings
and thee from my negligence.

Once I said to a scarecrow,
"You must be tired of standing in this lonely field."
And he said,
"The joy of scaring is a deep and lasting one, and I never tire of it."
Said I, after a minute of thought,
"It is true; for I too have known that joy."
Said he, "Only those who are stuffed with straw can know it."

Then I left him, not knowing whether he had complimented
or belittled me.
A year passed, during which the scarecrow turned philosopher.
And when I passed by him again, I saw two crows
building a nest under his hat.

One day there passed by a company of cats a wise dog.

And as he came near and saw that they were very intent and heeded him not, he stopped.

Then there arose in the midst of the company a large, grave cat and looked upon them and said, "Brethren, pray ye; and when ye have prayed again and yet again, nothing doubting, verily then it shall rain mice."

And when the dog heard this he laughed in his heart and turned from them saying, "O blind and foolish cats, has it not been written and have I not known and my fathers before me, that that which raineth for prayer and faith and supplication is not mice but bones."

Once there lived a man who had a valley full of needles. And one day the mother of Jesus came to him and said: "Friend, my son's garment is torn and I must needs mend it before he goeth to the temple. Wouldst thou not give me a needle?"

And he gave her not a needle, but he gave her a learned discourse on Giving and Taking to carry to her son before he should go to the temple.

A fox looked at his shadow at sunrise and said, "I will have a camel for lunch today." And all morning he went about looking for camels. But at noon he saw his shadow again — and he said, "A mouse will do."

Once there ruled in the distant city of Wirani a king who was both mighty and wise. And he was feared for his might and loved for his wisdom.

Now, in the heart of that city was a well, whose water was cool and crystalline, from which all the inhabitants drank, even the king and his courtiers; for there was no other well.

One night when all were asleep, a witch entered the city, and poured seven drops of strange liquid into the well, and said, "From this hour he who drinks this water shall become mad."

Next morning all the inhabitants, save the king and his lord chamberlain, drank from the well and became mad, even as the witch had foretold.

And during that day the people in the narrow streets and in the market places did naught but whisper to one another, "The king is mad. Our king and his lord chamberlain have lost their reason. Surely we cannot be ruled by a mad king. We must dethrone him."

That evening the king ordered a golden goblet to be filled from the well. And when it was brought to him he drank deeply, and gave it to his lord chamberlain to drink.

And there was great rejoicing in that distant city of Wirani, because its king and its lord chamberlain had regained their reason.

Last night I invented a new pleasure, and as I was giving it the first trial an angel and a devil came rushing toward my house. They met at my door and fought with each other over my newly created pleasure;
the one crying, "It is a sin!" — the other, "It is a virtue!"

Once when I was living in the heart of a pomegranate, I heard a seed saying, "Someday I shall become a tree, and the wind will sing in my branches, and the sun will dance on my leaves, and I shall be strong and beautiful through all the seasons."

Then another seed spoke and said, "When I was as young as you, I too held such views; but now that I can weigh and measure things,
I see that my hopes were vain."

And a third seed spoke also, "I see in us nothing that promises so great a future."

And a fourth said, "But what a mockery our life would be, without a greater future!"

Said a fifth, "Why dispute what we shall be, when we know not even what we are."

But a sixth replied, "Whatever we are, that we shall continue to be."

And a seventh said, "I have such a clear idea how everything will be, but I cannot put it into words."

Then an eight spoke—and a ninth—and a tenth—and then many—until all were speaking, and I could distinguish nothing for the many voices.

And so, I moved that very day into the heart of a quince, where the seeds are few and almost silent.

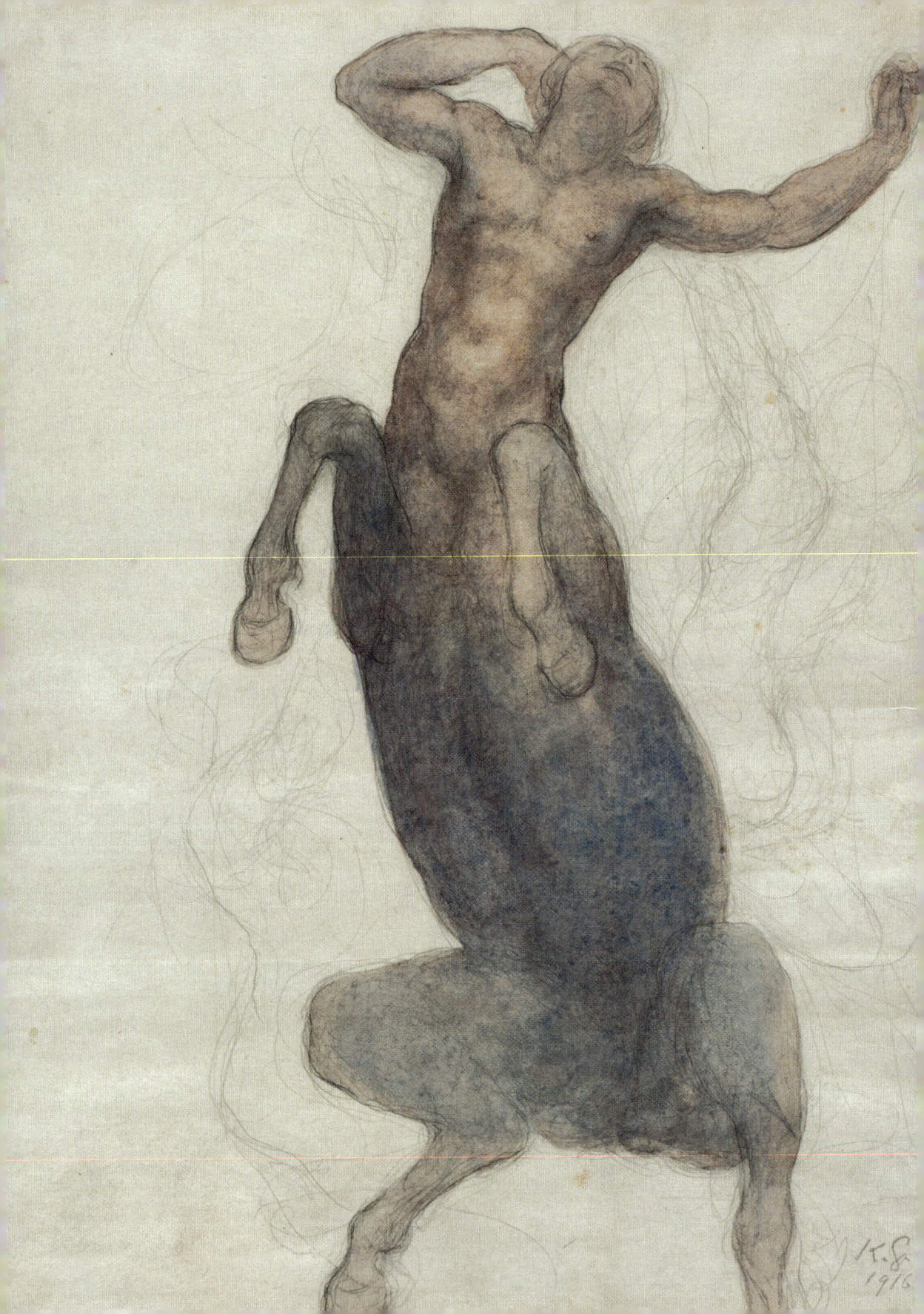

Once, as I was burying one of my dead selves,
the grave-digger came by and said to me,
"Of all those who come here to bury, you alone I like."

Said I, "You please me exceedingly, but why do you like me?"

"Because," said he, "They come weeping and go weeping —you only
come laughing and go laughing."

The Good God and the Evil God met on the mountain top.

The Good God said, "Good day to you, brother."

The Evil God did not answer.

And the Good God said, "You are in a bad humour today."

"Yes," said the Evil God, "for of late I have been often mistaken for you, called by your name, and treated as if I were you, and it ill-pleases me."

And the Good God said,
"But I too have been mistaken for you and called by your name."

The Evil God walked away cursing the stupidity of man.

Defeat, my Defeat, my solitude and my aloofness;
You are dearer to me than a thousand triumphs,
And sweeter to my heart than all world-glory.

Defeat, my Defeat, my shining sword and shield,
In your eyes I have read
That to be enthroned is to be enslaved,
And to be understood is to be levelled down,
And to be grasped is but to reach one's fullness
And like a ripe fruit to fall and be consumed.

Defeat, my Defeat, my deathless courage,
You and I shall laugh together with the storm,
And together we shall dig graves for all that die in us,
And we shall stand in the sun with a will,
And we shall be dangerous.

"Yea, we are twin brothers, O, Night;
for thou revealest space and I reveal my soul."

I HAVE SEEN A FACE WITH A THOUSAND COUNTENANCES, AND A FACE THAT WAS BUT A SINGLE COUNTENANCE AS IF HELD IN A MOULD.

I HAVE SEEN A FACE WHOSE SHEEN I COULD LOOK THROUGH TO THE UGLINESS BENEATH, AND A FACE WHOSE SHEEN I HAD TO LIFT TO SEE HOW BEAUTIFUL IT WAS.

I HAVE SEEN AN OLD FACE MUCH LINED WITH NOTHING, AND A SMOOTH FACE IN WHICH ALL THINGS WERE GRAVEN.

I KNOW FACES, BECAUSE I LOOK THROUGH THE FABRIC MY OWN EYE WEAVES, AND BEHOLD THE REALITY BENEATH.

REMEMBER ONLY THAT I SMILED.

In the shadow of the temple my friend and I saw a blind man sitting alone. And my friend said, "Behold the wisest man of our land."

Then I left my friend and approached the blind man and greeted him. And we conversed.

After a while I said, "Forgive my question; but since when has thou been blind?"

"From my birth," he answered.

Said I, "And what path of wisdom followest thou?"

Said he, "I am an astronomer."

Then he placed his hand upon his breast saying, "I watch all these suns and moons and stars."

Said a blade of grass to an autumn leaf,
"You make such a noise falling! You scatter all my winter dreams."

Said the leaf indignant, "Low-born and low-dwelling!
Songless, peevish thing! You live not in the upper air and
you cannot tell the sound of singing."

Then the autumn leaf lay down upon the earth and slept. And when spring
came she waked again — and she was a blade of grass.

And when it was autumn and her winter sleep was upon her, and above her
through all the air the leaves were falling, she muttered to herself, "O
these autumn leaves! They make such noise!
They scatter all my winter dreams."

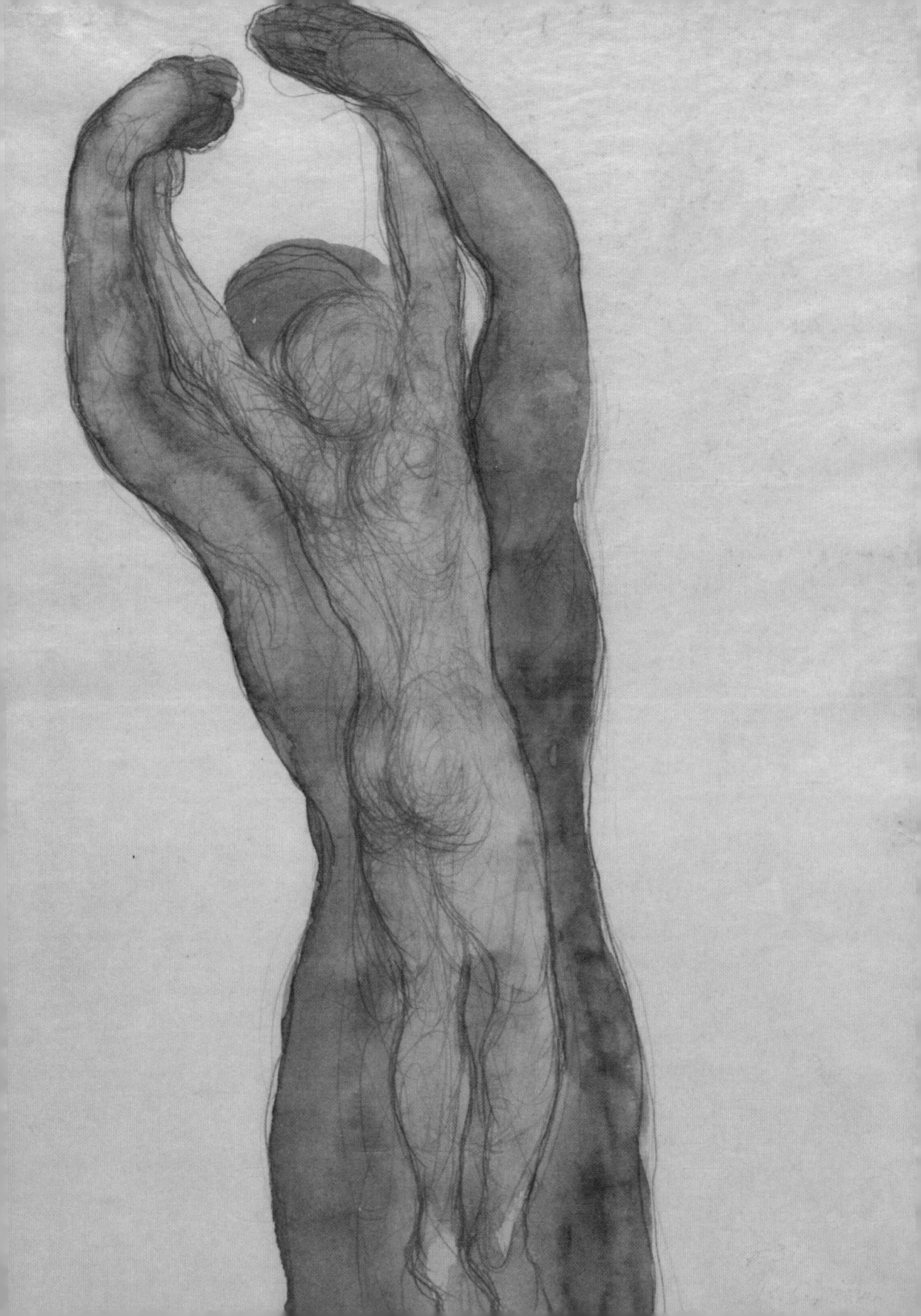

Said the Eye one day, "I see beyond these valleys a mountain veiled with blue mist. Is it not beautiful?"

The Ear listened, and after listening intently awhile, said, "But where is any mountain? I do not hear it."

Then the Hand spoke and said, "I am trying in vain to feel it or touch it, and I can find no mountain."

And the Nose said, "There is no mountain, I cannot smell it."

Then the Eye turned the other way, and they all began to talk together about the Eye's strange delusion. And they said, "Something must be the matter with the Eye."

When my Sorrow was born, I nursed it with care,
and watched over it with loving tenderness.

And my Sorrow grew like all living things, strong and beautiful
and full of wondrous delights.

And we loved one another, my Sorrow and I, and we loved the
world about us; for Sorrow had a kindly heart and mine was kindly
with Sorrow.

I, A HUMAN CHAOS, A NEBULA OF CONFUSED ELEMENTS, I MOVE AMONGST
FINISHED WORLDS — PEOPLES OF COMPLETE LAWS AND PURE ORDER, WHOSE
THOUGHTS ARE ASSORTED, WHOSE DREAMS ARE ARRANGED, AND WHOSE
VISIONS ARE ENROLLED AND REGISTERED.

THEIR VIRTUES, O GOD, ARE MEASURED, THEIR SINS ARE WEIGHED, AND EVEN
THE COUNTLESS THINGS THAT PASS IN THE DIM TWILIGHT OF NEITHER SIN
NOR VIRTUE ARE RECORDED AND CATALOGUED ...

... BUT WHY SHOULD I BE HERE, O GOD, I A GREEN SEED OF UNFULFILLED
PASSION, A MAD TEMPEST THAT SEEKETH NEITHER EAST NOR WEST, A
BEWILDERED FRAGMENT FROM A BURNT PLANET?

WHY AM I HERE, O GOD OF LOST SOULS,
THOU WHO ART LOST AMONGST THE GODS?

YOU ARE YOUR OWN FORERUNNER, AND THE TOWERS YOU HAVE BUILT ARE BUT THE FOUNDATION OF YOUR GIANT-SELF. AND THAT SELF TOO SHALL BE A FOUNDATION.

Always have we been our own forerunners, and always shall we be. And all that we have gathered and shall gather shall be but seeds for fields yet unploughed. We are the fields and the ploughmen, the gatherers and the gathered.

O love, whose lordly hand
Has bridled my desires,
And raised my hunger and my thirst
To dignity and pride,
Let not the strong in me and the constant
Eat the bread or drink the wine
That tempt my weaker self.

Let me rather starve
And let my heart parch with thirst,
And let me die and perish,
Ere I stretch my hand
To a cup you did not fill,
Or a bowl you did not bless.

And he said, "Nay, my friend, you knocked at the gate of my silences and received but a trifle. For who would not leave a kingdom for a forest where the seasons sing and dance ceaselessly? Many are those who have given their kingdom for less than solitude and the sweet fellowship of aloneness. Countless are the eagles who descend from the upper air to live with moles that they may know the secrets of the earth. There are those who renounce the kingdom of dreams that they may not seem distant from the dreamless. And those who renounce the kingdom of nakedness and cover their souls that others may not be ashamed in beholding truth uncovered and beauty unveiled. And greater yet than all of these is he who renounces the kingdom of sorrow that he may not seem proud and vainglorious."

Then rising he leaned upon his reed and said, "Go now to the great city and sit at its gate and watch all those who enter into it and those who go out. And see that you find him who, though born a king, is without kingdom; and him who though ruled in flesh rules in spirit — though neither he nor his subjects know this; and him also who but seems to rule yet is in truth slave of his own slaves."

After he had said these things, he smiled on me, and there were a thousand dawns upon his lips. Then he turned and walked away into the heart of the forest.

And the cat purred, "Only a slave restores a crown that has fallen."

In my wanderings I once saw upon an island a man-headed, iron-hoofed monster who ate of the earth and drank of the sea incessantly. And for a long while I watched him. Then I approached him and said, "Have you never enough; is your hunger never satisfied and your thirst never quenched?"

And he answered saying, "Yes, I am satisfied, nay, I am weary of eating and drinking; but I am afraid that tomorrow there will be no more earth to eat and no more sea to drink."

One nightfall a man travelling on horseback towards the sea reached an inn by the roadside. He dismounted and, confident in man and night like all riders towards the sea, he tied his horse to a tree beside the door and entered into the inn.

At midnight, when all were asleep, a thief came and stole the traveller's horse.

In the morning the man awoke and discovered that his horse was stolen. And he grieved for his horse, and that a man had found it in his heart to steal.

Then his fellow lodgers came and stood around him and began to talk.

And the first man said, "How foolish of you to tie your horse outside the stable."

And the second said, "Still more foolish, without even hobbling the horse!"

And the third man said, "It is stupid at best to travel to the sea on horseback."

And the fourth said, "Only the indolent and the slow of foot own horses."

Then the traveller was much astonished. At last he cried, "My friends, because my horse was stolen, you have hastened one and all to tell me my faults and my shortcomings. But strange, not one word of reproach have you uttered about the man who stole my horse."

Four poets were sitting around a bowl of punch that stood on a table.

Said the first poet, "Methinks I see with my third eye the fragrance of this wine hovering in space like a cloud of birds in an enchanted forest."

The second poet raised his head and said, "With my inner ear I can hear those mist-birds singing. And the melody holds my heart as the white rose imprisons the bee within her petals."

The third poet closed his eyes and stretched his arm upwards, and said, "I touch them with my hand. I feel their wings, like the breath of a sleeping fairy, brushing against my fingers."

Then the fourth poet rose and lifted up the bowl, and he said, "Alas, friends! I am too dull of sight and of hearing and of touch. I cannot see the fragrance of this wine, nor hear its song, nor feel the beating of its wings. I perceive but the wine itself. Now therefore must I drink it, that it may sharpen my senses and raise me to your blissful heights."

And putting the bowl to his lips, he drank the punch to the very last drop.

The three poets, with their mouths open, looked at him aghast, and there was a thirsty yet unlyrical hatred in their eyes.

Said the weather-cock to the wind, "How tedious and monotonous you are!
Can you not blow any other way but in my face?
You disturb my God-given stability."

And the wind did not answer. It only laughed in space.

Once the elders of the city of Aradus presented themselves before the king and besought of him a decree to forbid to men all wine and all intoxicants within their city.

And the king turned his back upon them and went out from them laughing.

Then the elders departed in dismay.

At the door of the palace they met the lord chamberlain. And the lord chamberlain observed that they were troubled, and he understood their case.

Then he said, "Pity, my friends! Had you found the king drunk, surely he would have granted you your petition."

Portrait of Kahlil Gibran by L C Penny

Out of my deeper heart a bird rose and flew skywards.
Higher and higher did it rise, yet larger and larger did it grow.
At first it was but like a swallow, then a lark, then an eagle,
then as vast as a spring cloud, and then it filled the starry heavens.
Out of my heart a bird flew skywards. And it waxed larger as it flew.
Yet it left not my heart.
O my faith, my untamed knowledge, how shall I fly to your height and see
with you man's larger self pencilled upon the sky?
How shall I turn this sea within me into mist,
and move with you in space immeasurable?
How can a prisoner within the temple behold its golden domes?
How shall the heart of a fruit be stretched to envelop the fruit also?
O my faith, I am in chains behind these bars of silver and ebony,
and I cannot fly with you.
Yet out of my heart you rise skyward, and it is my heart that holds you,
and I shall be content.

Four frogs sat upon a log that lay floating on the edge of a river. Suddenly the log was caught by the current and swept slowly down the stream. The frogs were delighted and absorbed, for never before had they sailed.

At length the first frog spoke, and said, "This is indeed a most marvellous log. It moves as if alive. No such log was ever known before."

Then the second frog spoke, and said, "Nay, my friend, the log is like other logs, and does not move. It is the river that is walking to the sea and carries us and the log with it."

And the third frog spoke, and said, "It is neither the log nor the river that moves. The moving is in our thinking. For without thought nothing moves."

And the three frogs began to wrangle about what was really moving. The quarrel grew hotter and louder, but they could not agree.

Then they turned to the fourth frog, who up to this time had been listening attentively but holding his peace, and they asked his opinion.

And the fourth frog said, "Each of you is right, and none of you is wrong. The moving is in the log and the water and our thinking also."

And the three frogs became very angry, for none of them was willing to admit that his was not the whole truth, and that the other two were not wholly wrong.

Then a strange thing happened. The three frogs got together and pushed the fourth frog off the log into the river.

Said a sheet of snow-white paper, "Pure was I created, and pure will I remain for ever. I would rather be burnt and turn to white ashes than suffer darkness to touch me or the unclean to come near me."

The ink-bottle heard what the paper was saying, and it laughed in its dark heart; but it never dared to approach her. And the multicoloured pencils heard her also, and they too never came near her.

And the snow-white sheet of paper did remain pure and chaste for ever, pure and chaste — and empty.

Once a man unearthed in his field a marble statue of great beauty. And he took it to a collector who loved all beautiful things and offered it to him for sale, and the collector bought it for a large price. And they parted.

And as the man walked home with his money he thought, and he said to himself, "How much life this money means! How can anyone give all this for a dead carved stone buried and undreamed of in the earth for a thousand years?"

And now the collector was looking at his statue, and he was thinking, and he said to himself, "What beauty! What life! The dream of what a soul! — and fresh with the sweet sleep of a thousand years. How can anyone give all this for money, dead and dreamless?"

A fish said to another fish, "Above this sea of ours there is another sea, with creatures swimming in it — and they live there even as we live here."

The fish replied, "Pure fancy! Pure fancy! When you know that everything that leaves our sea by even an inch, and stays out of it, dies. What proof have you of other lives in other seas?"

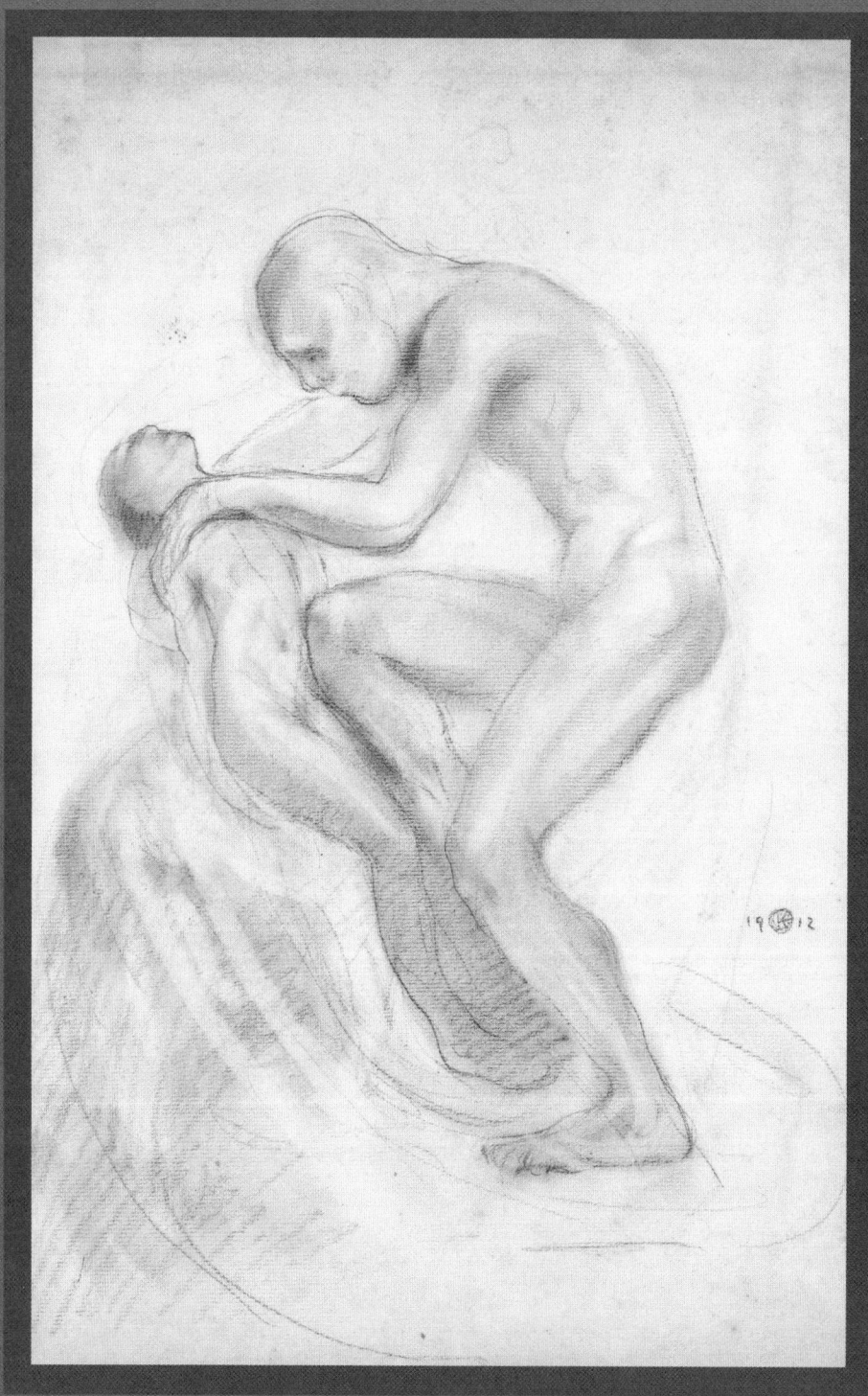

Beyond my solitude is another solitude, and to him who dwells therein my aloneness is a crowded market place and my silence a confusion of sounds.

Beyond these hills is a grove of enchantment and to him who dwells therein my peace is but a whirlwind and my enchantment an illusion.

Beyond this burdened self, lives my freer self; and to him my dreams are a battle fought in twilight and my desires the rattling of bones.

Too young am I and too outraged to be my freer self.

And how shall I become my freer self unless I slay my burdened selves, or unless all men become free?

How shall the eagle in me soar against the sun until my fledglings leave the nest which I with my own beak have built for them?

After saying these things, the Forerunner covered his face with his hands and wept bitterly. For he knew in his heart that love humiliated in its nakedness is greater than love that seeks triumph in disguise; and he was ashamed.

But suddenly he raised his head, and like one waking from sleep he outstretched his arms and said, "Night is over, and we children of night must die when dawn comes leaping upon the hills; and out of our ashes a mightier love shall rise. And it shall laugh in the sun, and it shall be deathless."

Pages 1, 4, 19, 20, 22, 39, 40, 41, 59, 60, 61, 102, 159, 161, 199, 200, 219:
A license to feature these paintings in this publication was granted to the publisher by the Gibran National Committee, address: P.O. Box 116-5375, Beirut, Lebanon; Phone & Fax: +961-1-396916 and +961-1-396921; E-Mail: committee@gibrankhalilgibran.org.
The Gibran National Committee is a not-for-profit organization holding the exclusive rights to manage Khalil Gibran's copyright in and to his literary and artistic works including the works featured in this publication.

Pages 2, 21, 42, 62, 79, 80, 81, 82, 99, 100, 101, 119, 120, 121, 122, 139, 140, 141, 142, 160, 162, 179, 180, 181, 182, 202:
A license to feature these paintings in this publication was granted to the publisher by Telfair Museums, Savannah, Georgia.